student

WORKBOOK

GCSE Schools History Project

Enquiry in Depth: The American West, 1840–95

John Collingwood

Philip Allan, an imprint of Hodder Education, an Hachette UK company, Market Place, Deddington, Oxfordshire OX15 0SE

Orders
Bookpoint Ltd, 130 Milton Park, Abingdon, Oxfordshire, OX14 4SB
tel: 01235 827827 fax: 01235 400401 e-mail: education@bookpoint.co.uk

Lines are open 9.00 a.m.–5.00 p.m., Monday to Saturday, with a 24-hour message answering service. You can also order through the Philip Allan website: www.philipallan.co.uk

ISBN 978-1-84489-822-0

Printed in Spain

Hachette UK's policy is to use papers that are natural, renewable and recyclable products and made from wood grown in sustainable forests. The logging and manufacturing processes are expected to conform to the environmental regulations of the country of origin.

P02247

Introduction

This workbook is designed to help you prepare for the GCSE examination module Enquiry in Depth: The American West, 1840–95. The content is divided into eight topics, the first seven of which provide notes on an important aspect of this enquiry in depth. The last topic provides an overview of the whole content and emphasises how all the developments covered in this book happened simultaneously over a period of about 55 years.

Within each of the first seven topics you will find:

- **a summary of essential knowledge**, focusing on changes during the period of study and the main factors that have influenced those changes. These summaries are not intended to cover all the details of a particular theme and should be used with your class notes and textbook.
- **questions and exercises**, which are designed to help you learn and/or revise each topic and also practise the skills that are essential for the examination:
  - — the analysis and evaluation of sources
  - — the writing of extended answers, using your own knowledge of each topic

Spaces are provided for your answers, which give you some idea of how long each answer should be. The questions are structured so that they increase in difficulty within each topic.

Source questions

When answering source questions there are two important points to remember.

First, don't just **describe** what a written source says, or a picture shows. Try to draw an **inference** or make a **deduction** about the overall meaning or significance of the source. For example, you could be given a picture source such as the one in Topic 4, The homesteaders, Question 15, and asked: 'What does Source A suggest about the lives of homesteaders in the late 1800s?'

Many candidates make the mistake of just describing in detail what they can see in the picture. Better candidates start by making an inference and then referring to details to support what they have said, such as 'Source A suggests that homesteaders still had hard lives in the late 1800s. You can tell this because you can see…'.

Second, if the question tells you to 'use the **source** and your own **knowledge** in your answer' — then make sure you do use both. Try to get into the habit of using the source first and referring to it by its name, i.e. 'Source A' or 'Source B' and so on.

Extended writing

The last questions in each topic are designed as 'extended writing' or essay exercises. You should write your answers to these questions on separate paper. You should end these answers with a separate conclusion. However, do not just summarise what you have already said; you should state an opinion in answer to the question set and support it with a strong point based on your knowledge of the topic.

Topic 1 The Plains Indians

The Indians are the original inhabitants of North America, which is why today they prefer to be called **Native Americans**. The first Europeans to visit the New World wrongly called them 'Indians', and this name is still widely used.

There were, and still are, many different tribes — some, like the Sioux, so large that they are sometimes called 'nations'. Early in the nineteenth century the Sioux nation was thought to consist of about 20,000 people.

The different tribes often led different lives depending on their environment. This topic is about the Plains Indians who lived in the central part of North America in a region known as the Great Plains. This region is shown on the map below.

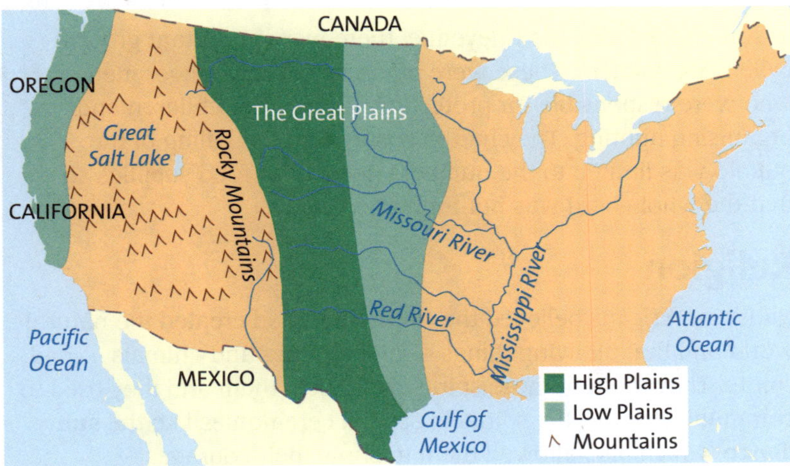

The Great Plains in 1840

At least 30 tribes lived on the Great Plains. The largest of these tribes were the Apache, Arapaho, Cheyenne, Comanche, Crow, Kiowa and Sioux. These tribes were further divided into bands, each with their own chief.

The way of life of the Plains Indians

The Plains Indians were **nomads** — people who do not live in one permanent place. There were two main reasons for this nomadic way of life:

- They depended on the buffalo for food, clothing, covers for tipis and tools — in fact, all their everyday needs. As the buffalo herds kept moving across the Plains, the Indians followed them.
- Their nomadic way of life was also connected to their beliefs about land. The Indians believed land was provided by the Great Spirit for all living creatures to share. Therefore, they believed no one should ever live permanently on one piece of land because they would be claiming it for themselves.

Family life

The Native Americans were skilled at adapting to the tough environment in which they lived and many features of their family life reflect this:

- Families who were related to one another travelled together in groups called bands. These bands of about 100–500 people gave safety in numbers and made hunting easier. They also ensured children would always have someone to look after them if their parents died.

- Indians looked after their children well and it was rare for parents to punish them. Children were taught to respect and to be polite to older people. They were also taught to value all living things because they were thought to have spirits of their own. As they grew up, both boys and girls had to learn skills vital for survival. Boys learnt about hunting and warfare; girls had to learn how to make clothes from buffalo skins, how to prepare food and, most important of all, how to take down the tipi swiftly and pack up the family's belongings when the time came to move camp.
- A family of eight to ten people lived in a tipi. Although tipis appeared primitive to white travellers, they were constructed so that they not only provided the family with a cool home for summer and a warm one for winter, but they could also be taken down quickly. This was vital as the band had to keep track of the buffalo when the herds moved on. A whole camp could be packed up and on the move in less than an hour. The tipi poles were used to make a **travois** — a kind of sledge for carrying belongings.
- Sometimes, men would be killed when hunting or in battle. When this happened, their wives would be taken in by other men — even if they already had a wife. This was another way of making sure everyone was looked after and made sense in a society in which women often outnumbered men. However, this practice of **polygamy** was, to white Christians, proof that the Indians were 'savages'.
- The elderly were greatly respected. They passed on the history of the tribe and their views were always listened to in Indian councils. Unfortunately, life on the Plains was often a struggle and when the old became too weak to travel they were left behind. The survival of the whole band depended on keeping up with the buffalo.

Organisation

Daily life within a band was based more on customs and tradition than any system of formal authority. A council of elders who met with the chief normally made decisions. In the summer, the bands within a tribe would meet up for special ceremonies and the chiefs of all the bands would hold a special council. However, individual bands frequently ignored decisions made during this special council.

In some tribes, like the Cheyenne, there were important groups called dog soldiers. These were made up of the younger men who were responsible for protecting women and children and organising hunting. They had to ensure that the killing of the buffalo was limited to the numbers needed for food supplies so that the whole herd was not frightened away.

Religion

Native Americans believed the Great Spirit had created the natural world and that all living things — plants, trees and animals — had spirits. They thought these spirits could help them and they tried to communicate with the spirits in special ceremonies like the **sun dance**, which also allowed them to show their courage.

Some people in the tribes — called shamen or medicine men — had special powers that allowed them to communicate with the spirits and interpret dreams and visions. When someone died, special ceremonies were held. Indians believed the spirit of the dead person went to the 'happy hunting ground'.

Warfare

Indians did fight one another, but this usually only involved small groups carrying out raids on bands in enemy tribes. They did not attack in order to conquer other people or take over land. Their motive was sometimes revenge or a matter of honour, but normally the main goal was to steal horses. Horses were important to the Indians. They pulled the travois and so helped when moving camp, but, even more importantly, horses made it easier to hunt buffalo.

Indians saw no point in making a stand and fighting to the death. If the fighting went badly, they retreated so they would not risk being killed. This appeared cowardly to whites. Sometimes, Indians would kill their enemies, but a greater sign of bravery was to 'count coup' — ride up to an enemy and strike him with a stick. Special feathers were awarded for this and the more successful a warrior was, the more feathers he wore in his hair.

The greatest fear in battle was to be scalped because Indians believed that if your enemy had your scalp he also had your spirit. This meant you would not go to the 'happy hunting ground' when you died. Native Americans took the scalps of their enemies so that they would not meet up with them again after death. Scalps were often hung from tipis or attached to a warrior's clothing. White people were appalled by the taking of scalps and saw it as further proof that Indians were 'savages'.

The attitudes of whites towards Indians

Some whites, like George Catlin, the painter, got to know Indians well and understood their customs. Catlin travelled in the West in the 1830s before there was a lot of fighting between Indians and white people. He admired the way Indians were able to adapt to life on the Plains.

Many whites, however, thought Indians were holding up progress because they did not cultivate the land they lived on. Others saw them as 'savages'. This was due to Indian customs that they did not try to understand, such as taking scalps, leaving old people behind when moving camp, the practice of polygamy and rituals like the sun dance. Some of the whites wanted the Indians to be exterminated.

Topic 1 The Plains Indians

Use the information provided, your class notes and your textbook to answer the following questions.

1 The following key words and phrases are defined in the table. Write each key word next to the correct definition.

- Dog soldiers
- Band
- Nomads
- Travois
- Counting coup
- Sun dance
- Medicine man
- Polygamy
- Native Americans

2 Give **two** reasons why the Plains Indians followed a nomadic way of life.

1

Definition	Key word or phrase
Someone who could communicate with spirits and interpret visions	
A title given to people who have no fixed home and keep moving from place to place	
What Indians prefer to be known as today	
A special group in some tribes who protected women and children and organised hunting	
A special ceremony in which a brave tried to communicate with the spirits	
A number of related families who travelled around as a group	
The practice of a man having more than one wife	
An act of bravery that involved striking an enemy with a stick	
A sledge made from tipi poles and used to carry belongings when moving camp	

2

Questions

3 Describe **three** ways in which the Native Americans used parts of the buffalo.

4 What skills did
a boys
b girls
learn as they grew up?

5 In what ways did the tipi provide an ideal home for the Plains Indians?

6 Why did the Plains Indians practise polygamy? Give more than one reason.

7 Why were old people sometimes left behind when a band moved camp?

8 How were tribes organised and governed?

3

4a

b

5

6

7

8

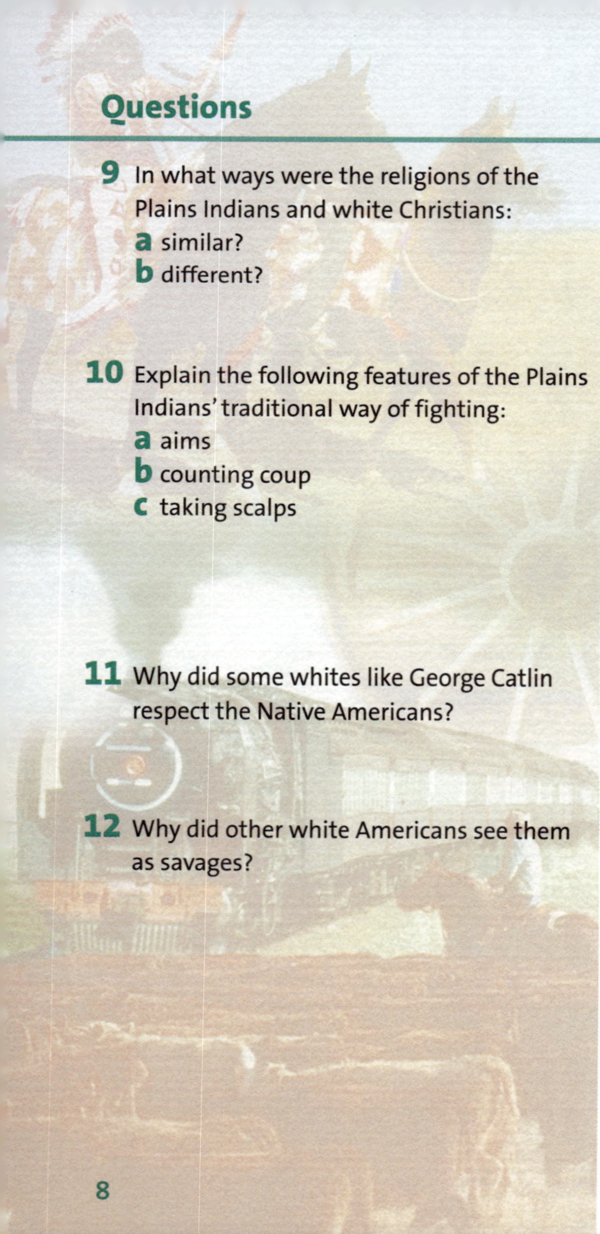

Questions

9 In what ways were the religions of the Plains Indians and white Christians:
a similar?
b different?

10 Explain the following features of the Plains Indians' traditional way of fighting:
a aims
b counting coup
c taking scalps

11 Why did some whites like George Catlin respect the Native Americans?

12 Why did other white Americans see them as savages?

9a

b

10a

b

c

11

12

Questions

Source A

The tepee is much better to live in; always warm in winter, cool in summer; easy to move. The white man builds big house, like big cage, shuts out sun, can never move; always sick. Indians and animals know better how to live than white men.

By Chief Flying Hawk of the Sioux (1852–1931)

Source B

The North American Indian in his native state is an honest, faithful, brave, warlike, cruel — yet thoughtful and religious being. I pronounce them, by nature a kind and hospitable people.

From *Letters about the North American Indians* by George Catlin, published in 1841

Source C

The Indians are children. Their wars, treaties, crafts, comforts all belong to the very lowest ages of human existence. Squalid, conceited, proud and worthless...they will in time give the world relief by dying out of it.

From *An Overland Journey from New York to San Francisco* by Horace Greeley, published in 1859

Source questions

13 What does Source A tell you about the way of life of the Plains Indians?

- Quote details from the source to show what you can learn from it about the Native Americans.
- Try to make at least one inference (deduction) from the details in the source.

14 Study Sources B and C. What different impressions of the Plains Indians do you get from these sources?

- You must explain *how* they differ, not why.
- Compare details in *both* sources — do not just describe one.

13

14

Questions

15 Why do you think Sources B and C show different views of the Native Americans? Explain your answer using Sources B and C and your own knowledge.

- You need to give *reasons* for the differences. Do not repeat *how* the sources differ.

Extended writing

On separate paper, write a short essay in answer to the following question.

16 How important were differences in attitudes to land in explaining why some white people saw the Native Americans as 'savages'?

15

16 You could include the following in your answer and any other information of your own:

- White people thought land should be used and developed.
- Indian men could take more than one wife.
- Old people were sometimes left behind when Indians moved camp.

Topic 2 The first white people in the West

The first white people to travel to the West did not settle on the Great Plains. They wanted to go further west. This topic looks at four groups of people who, for different reasons, travelled to the far West in the 1830s and 1840s: the mountain men, farmers, miners and the Mormons.

The mountain men

These men were hunters. They went west to hunt and trap animals for their furs. Although they left no permanent mark, they did help the settlement of the West in other ways:

- They told stories about the fertile lands that were beyond the Rocky Mountains. These stories encouraged other white people to go west.
- Many mountain men, like Jim Bridger, acted as paid guides for wagon trains, helping them to find their way through the mountains.

Farmers

These people brought their families west mainly for the good farmland in California and Oregon that they had heard about. While this 'pulled' them westwards, other factors 'pushed' them:

- In 1837, an economic depression hit the eastern USA. Banks collapsed and people lost their savings. Wages fell and unemployment rose.
- Farmers along the Mississippi Valley were also hit hard by falling wheat prices.

For many, going west was a way to escape from all of this. These early settlers travelled across the Plains and mountains in the early 1840s in increasing numbers — from about 1,000 in 1843 to about 55,000 by 1850.

Difficulties and dangers

The journey west was extremely tough. The covered wagons the settlers travelled in often broke down on the rough trails. Even on the Plains they could only cover about 32 km (20 miles) a day, and through the mountains progress was much slower. Food and water shortages, together with disease, especially cholera, meant many died along the way — around 34,000 in the period between 1840 and 1860. The journey from Independence, Missouri, to California or Oregon was nearly 4,000 km and took over 6 months. It had to be completed by mid-November because heavy snowfalls made the mountains impassable in winter.

Miners

Miners went west when gold was discovered in California in 1848. Most miners travelled in 1849 and were known as the '49ers. Mining towns in California and the Rocky Mountains were lawless places.

- The towns grew quickly as thousands of miners arrived, but there were no sheriffs or marshals to keep order.
- 'Claim jumping' — people trying to steal land where gold had been discovered — was common.

- Mining towns attracted criminal types, and drinking and gambling were common.
- There were many different races present and fighting between them often broke out. Many Chinese and Mexicans were murdered.
- Very few people found large amounts of gold and this led to disappointment, boredom and more fighting.

In order to keep some kind of peace, the miners set up their own miners' courts to sort out quarrels. These were fairly successful, but sometimes groups of vigilantes took the law into their own hands. They often acted as judge, jury and executioner, even when there was little evidence against the accused. Many innocent people were hanged and the vigilantes became more feared than the actual criminals.

By 1852, the surface diggings in California had been exhausted. Gradually, a large proportion of the miners returned home and some towns became ghost towns. However, the miners did help speed up the settlement of the West.

- Some towns, like San Francisco, became large and prosperous.
- The mining towns brought other people west, such as lawyers, traders and builders.
- The presence of many more people in the West by the 1850s speeded up the building of a railway right across America, which really opened up the West.

Discoveries of gold and silver in other parts of the West led to further, smaller gold rushes in Colorado and Nevada (1858–59), Montana (1862) and the Black Hills of Dakota (1874).

The Mormons

The reason why the Mormons went west was different. Their story began in a small town called Palmyra in New York State. A young man called Joseph Smith claimed that, in 1823, he had been visited by an angel who, 4 years later, revealed to him gold plates buried in a hillside. These plates gave a different version of the Old Testament and Smith was told that his mission was to restore the true Church of Jesus Christ in America and to prepare for the return of Christ to earth. The Mormon Church (The Church of Jesus Christ of Latter-Day Saints) was started in 1830 with just five members. Within a year, there were over 1,000 members. The Mormons tried to build their own community in three states, but each time were driven out: from **Ohio** (1831–37), **Missouri** (1838) and finally **Illinois** (1839–46).

Dislike of the Mormons

People disliked the Mormons for a variety of reasons:

- They resented the fact that the Mormons claimed to be God's 'chosen people' on earth.
- They were jealous of how successful the Mormons became as farmers.
- They were afraid because the number of Mormons was growing quickly.

Matters were brought to a head in Kirtland, Ohio, when the Mormon bank became bankrupt in 1837 and many non-Mormons (as well as many Mormons) lost all their savings. The failure of the bank was a consequence of the general economic depression of

1837 and other banks failed too, but for the people of Kirtland, it was the last straw and the Mormons were driven out.

They were given little chance of settling in Missouri, where rumours that the Mormons were friendly towards Indians and in favour of abolishing slavery led to violent attacks on their homes and, once again, they were forced out of the state.

A similar pattern developed in Illinois. The Mormons bought land and built up a town called Nauvoo; by 1844, over 10,000 inhabitants lived there. By this time, they had formed their own army (the Danites), and their power and influence seemed to be growing. In 1844, Joseph Smith announced that he had received a revelation from God that enabled Mormons to take more than one wife (**polygamy**). This would clearly make the number of Mormons increase more quickly and it created more hostility towards them. This resentment grew worse when Smith announced that he planned to run for president of the USA. With Illinois on the verge of civil war, Joseph Smith was arrested and murdered by a mob while in prison.

Brigham Young

After the death of Joseph Smith, Brigham Young became leader of the Mormons. This was a turning point in the story of the Mormon Church because Young decided that the only way they would be able to live in peace would be to move west, to an area of the Rocky Mountains that was outside the USA. They would find a remote spot where no one else would want to live. This would leave them free from political interference by the government and free from non-Mormon settlers.

Preparations began in the autumn of 1845 and, as attacks on their homes grew worse, the Mormon community of 15,000 people started out on the 2,400 km journey west in spring 1846. An advance group went on ahead to set up **Winter Quarters** on the banks of the Missouri River and plant crops that could be harvested by those coming later. Like all travellers at the time, the Mormons suffered great hardships on the journey and many died on the way. The group survived because of the organisational skills and tough leadership of Young, and in the summer of 1847 the first Mormons reached the valley of the Great Salt Lake.

Settlement in the Salt Lake Valley

The Mormons had many problems to overcome here in this desolate spot, but again, the vision and leadership of Brigham Young ensured that the community survived and thrived. They succeeded in 'making the desert bloom', just as Brigham Young had said they would. However, there were problems to be resolved:

- Land had to be shared out fairly to avoid disputes between people.
- The soil was dry and water from the lake too salty to drink.
- There were few trees for building homes.
- Young was determined that they would not have to depend on non-Mormons for anything.
- More Mormons with skills had to be helped to get to the Salt Lake Valley.

All these problems were solved by Brigham Young. Laws were made to ensure that no one could own the land or water; everyone would get a fair share. Irrigation channels were built to bring fresh water from the mountains and houses were built out of adobe (bricks made of dried clay). The Mormons had to make everything they needed themselves. Money would be set aside to help other Mormons from both the eastern USA and Europe make the long journey west. By the end of 1851, 33,000 Mormons from England alone were ready to travel. As more people arrived, new settlements were started in other parts of the valley.

Relations with the government

In 1848, the USA defeated Mexico in a short war and took over an area of Mexican territory including the Salt Lake Valley. Brigham Young wanted the area to be an independent state called Deseret, but a compromise was reached whereby it became the US territory of **Utah** (after the Ute Indians who lived in the area), with Young as its first governor.

The Mormons' relationship with the rest of the USA was always strained. As more and more settlers moved to California, the Mormons set up supply depots for them, but also charged them tolls (taxes) for crossing their territory. The Mormons appeared to be friendlier towards Indians than white non-Mormons. This was considered strange behaviour by other whites and some people believed they were arming the Indians so that they could attack travellers. It was also claimed that US laws were ignored in Utah and that Brigham Young used the Danites to crush any opposition to his rule.

In 1857, the government decided to assert its authority by sending a non-Mormon governor, with 1,500 troops, to Utah to replace Young. This created an atmosphere of fear and tension in Utah and the Mormons saw this as an invasion designed to crush their communities. One consequence of this was the **Mountain Meadows Massacre** of 1857, when 140 migrants in a wagon train were attacked and killed. The Mormon leaders blamed the Indians, but many believed the Danites were responsible. However, it made the government realise that if more bloodshed were to be avoided, another compromise was needed. The Mormons agreed to accept a non-Mormon governor and the government promised it would make no attempt to interfere in their religion or way of life. Despite this, Brigham Young remained the most powerful and influential figure in Mormon life until his death in 1877.

Finally, Utah was made a new state of the USA in 1896, and the Mormons agreed to abolish polygamy. Today, more than 2 million people live in Utah and the majority of them are Mormons. Salt Lake City is a modern, prosperous city of over 180,000 people.

Topic 2 The first white people in the West

Use the information provided, your class notes and your textbook to answer the following questions.

1 The following key words and phrases are defined in the table. Write each key word next to the correct definition.

- Mountain men
- The '49ers
- Claim jumping
- Miners' courts
- Vigilantes
- Deseret
- Utah
- Adobe
- Mountain Meadows

1

Definition	Key word or phrase
When one miner tried to claim ownership of land where another miner had discovered gold	
A place where a massacre of travellers took place in 1857	
The name given to people who went west to California in search of gold	
Men who took the law into their own hands and acted as judge, jury and executioner of criminals	
Men who went west as hunters and fur trappers but later acted as guides for wagon trains	
The name given to the Mormon territory and state by the government	
These unofficial courts dealt with quarrels between miners	
The Mormons used these bricks made of clay to build their first homes	
The name the Mormons wanted to give to their own state	

2 How did mountain men make a living?

2

Questions

3 Describe **two** things mountain men did to help the settlement of the West.

4 Describe **one** 'pull' factor and **one** 'push' factor that encouraged farmers to go west.

5 What sort of difficulties and dangers faced people travelling west at this time?

6 Give **three** reasons why early mining towns were such lawless places.

7 Describe **two** things miners did to try to solve the problem of law and order.

8 Did the vigilantes improve law and order in mining towns or make it worse? Explain your answer.

3

4 'Pull' factor

'Push' factor

5

6

7

8

Questions

9 Describe **two** ways in which miners helped the settlement of the West.

9

10 Study the map, which shows the movements of the Mormons. Put **dates** in the appropriate boxes to show when the following things happened:

- Joseph Smith was first visited by an angel.
- The Mormons set up their first community.
- They were driven out of here after just one year.
- They left this state after seven difficult years.
- They finally settled in this place.

10

The movements of the Mormons

Questions

11 Describe **three** reasons why people in Ohio, Illinois and Missouri disliked the Mormons.

12 a How did Joseph Smith die in 1844?
b Who took over as leader?

13 Why was this change in leadership a turning point in the story of the Mormons?

14 Why did Young decide to settle in the Salt Lake Valley? Explain your answer.

15 How did Young ensure that there would be sufficient food supplies for the long journey west?

Topic 2 The first white people in the West

11

12a

b

13

14

15

Questions

16 Use the table to list **five** problems the Mormons had to overcome when they settled in the Salt Lake Valley. In the second column, give the solution they came up with.

17 Give **two** reasons why relations between the Mormons and other Americans became strained during the 1850s.

18 Describe briefly the events before and after the Mountain Meadows Massacre of 1857.

16

Problems the Mormons had	How they were solved

17

18

Questions

19 Complete the table by writing the following phrases and statements in the correct spaces. (Some spaces have more than one correct statement that applies to them.)

- Helped San Francisco to grow rapidly
- Heard stories about good farmland
- The Salt Lake Valley
- Told stories about good land west of the Rocky Mountains
- To escape persecution
- The Rocky Mountains
- Set up farming settlements in Oregon and California
- California and the Rocky Mountains
- Created the successful state of Utah in the Rockies
- To hunt animals and sell their furs
- To look for gold and get rich
- Other traders went west and set up stores to supply their needs
- To be free to follow their own religion in peace
- California and Oregon
- Acted as guides for early wagon trains going through the Rockies

19

Type of settler	**Destination**	**Reason for going west**	**How they helped the settlement of the West**
Mountain men			
Farmers			
Miners			
The Mormons			

Questions

Source questions

20 How useful is Source A in helping you to understand why the Mormons moved west in the 1840s? Explain your answer using the source and your own knowledge.

- Use details in the source to support your answer.
- Use your knowledge to show the limitations of the source, i.e. other reasons why the Mormons went west, which cannot be seen in this source.

TOPFOTO

Source A

A cartoon from the 1840s in America making fun of Mormon family life

20

Source B

A Mormon family on their way to the Salt Lake Valley in 1867

PETER NEWARK'S WESTERN AMERICANA

21 What can you learn from Source B about the people who went to join the Mormon community after it had been established in the West?

- Refer to details in the picture and say what can be learned from them.
- Try to make at least one deduction from the overall impression it gives you.

Extended writing

On separate paper, write a short essay in answer to the following question.

22 How important was the leadership of Brigham Young in the establishment of a successful Mormon community in the West by 1890? Explain your answer.

21

22 You could include the following in your answer and any other information of your own:

- Joseph Smith started the Mormon Church in 1830.
- The Mormons faced lots of problems when they arrived in the Salt Lake Valley.
- A massacre occurred at Mountain Meadows in 1857.

Topic 3 Cattlemen and cowboys

Cattle ranching began in Texas in the 1830s. When the American Civil War ended in 1865, there were so many cattle in Texas that the price of beef fell to $4 a head. Cattlemen realised that if they could get their herds to the railway, which was being built across the country to the West, their cattle could be sent to northern cities like Chicago where they were worth $40 — so began the cattle drives.

The cattle trails

The first of these was the Sedalia Trail. It took about 3 months to take a herd of between 2,000 and 3,000 cattle from Texas to Sedalia and there were problems along the way. Outlaws called rustlers often tried to steal cattle. Farmers near the trail did not like the Texan Longhorn cattle going near their farms because:

- they trampled on and ate crops
- they carried a disease called Texas fever to which they were immune, but other breeds of cattle were not

To avoid these problems, other cattle trails were developed further west — the Chisholm and Western Trails. Two men, **Charles Goodnight** and **Oliver Loving**, opened yet another trail to take cattle to the army forts and Indian reservations on the western Plains. Although shortage of water was a problem on this drive, it showed there was an alternative market to the cities of the East and North, and others later followed their example.

A key individual who helped overcome the problems of the trails and developed the cattle business was **Joseph McCoy**. In 1867, he built the first 'cow town' at **Abilene**, a place where cattle sellers and buyers could meet and trade cattle safely. The town grew rapidly and thousands of cattle were traded there: 37,000 in 1867 increasing to 700,000 by 1871. As the railway moved further west, other cow towns were developed such as Ellsworth and Dodge City. By 1885, 4 million cattle had passed through the cow towns.

Cattle ranching on the Plains

In the early 1870s, some cattlemen started to look for alternatives to the **long drives** up from Texas. They began to build ranches on the Great Plains, where there was free open land closer to the railway. **John Iliff** was one of the first to do this. He also began to experiment by cross-breeding his Longhorn cattle with English breeds. These produced more meat and milk than the Longhorns. Others copied his ideas and a **boom** period in cattle ranching began, which lasted to the mid-1880s.

The largest ranches on the Plains covered thousands of acres, but the land was not owned by anyone or fenced in. Cattle roamed freely on this **open range** and had to be branded to establish ownership. Owners of the biggest herds became known as **cattle barons**. Ranching on the Plains was much easier in the 1870s because by this time most of the Indians had been pushed on to reservations and the buffalo, which before had grazed on the open range, were being slaughtered in their thousands by white hunters. By 1880, over 4 million cattle were being kept on the northern Plains, but this boom period in the cattle business came to a rapid end in the mid-1880s.

The large ranches the cattle barons built included not only a home for their own family but also bunkhouses (living quarters) for the cowboys they employed, stables and barns. In fact, the cattlemen became the first whites to build permanent homes on the high Plains of Colorado, Nebraska, Wyoming and Montana. This encouraged other settlers to follow them. It also stimulated further development of the railway, which in turn made it easier for people to move there. In this way, the cattlemen and cowboys made a significant contribution to the development of the West.

The end of the cattle boom

The causes of the bust in the cattle business were as follows:

- There was a fall in demand for beef in the eastern cities, which led to lower prices. To reduce the supply of beef, cattlemen kept more of their cattle on the Plains rather than sending them for slaughter.
- This led to the problem of **overstocking**. There were too many cattle on the Plains in 1883 when a drought in the long, hot summer meant the grass did not grow and there was not enough food for the cattle. Another drought occurred in the summer of 1886.
- This was followed by the terrible winter of 1886–87, which killed thousands of cattle.

After this, cattlemen were forced to maintain a better balance between the number of cattle and the amount of grass available. This meant fencing in land so that grazing could be controlled more effectively, but fencing was expensive. Moreover, water was still vital and this was often a source of conflict. However, both problems were solved by two technical inventions:

- **Barbed wire** (developed by **Joseph Glidden** in 1874) had been first used by farmers, but now cattlemen found it a cheap and efficient form of fencing. It also stopped cattle wandering on to crops and so eased a cause of conflict between cattlemen and neighbouring farmers.
- **Wind pumps**, which brought water up from deep below the ground, meant that water could be provided in any fenced-off area. This brought an end to fights between cattlemen over the rights to rivers and water holes.

However, these changes were to have a profound effect on the lives of the cowboys.

The life of the cowboy

The cowboy's life has often been thought of as glamorous. This myth comes from:

- cheap paperback novels ('dime novels') written in the 1890s to entertain readers in the eastern USA
- the 'Wild West' shows of **William Cody (Buffalo Bill)** that toured American and European cities from the mid-1880s to 1912, performing battle scenes with cavalry against the Indians
- Hollywood films of the 1920s and 1930s, which were often based on the 'dime novels' of the 1890s

All of these made the life of the cowboy seem much more exciting than it really was. In reality, the cowboy's life centred on cattle. It was hard, often boring, and sometimes dangerous.

Why did men become cowboys?

Men became cowboys for a variety of reasons:

- many were black ex-slaves who wanted to get away from racism in the American South
- others were ex-soldiers who found it hard to settle after the Civil War
- some were young men who liked the outdoor life but thought farming was inferior
- in the West there were few other jobs — especially for men who were not well educated — and the pay on a long drive was good

What did cowboys do?

On the open range, the main jobs were:

- in winter, to patrol and make sure the cattle were safe in the snow and to rescue any that sank in mud — this was called 'riding the line' and was especially lonely
- in spring, to round up the cattle and brand new calves
- in summer, to round up the cattle again and take them on the long drive to the railway

Clothing

Clothing was specially adapted for being out in all weathers. For example, the wide-brimmed Stetson hat could protect the face from the sun in summer and in winter it could be pulled down to protect the ears. The bandana around the neck could be pulled up over the nose to give protection from dust when riding 'drag' (at the rear of the herd). The chaps worn over the trousers protected the legs from thorny vegetation, cold winds and injury in the case of a fall.

Difficulties on the long drive

- The drives could take up to 3 months and during this time the cowboys would sleep out in all weathers.
- Rivers swollen by heavy rain could be dangerous to cross.
- Trouble with rustlers or farmers occurred frequently.
- The worst difficulty was having to cope with **stampedes**. Sounds at night could spark off a stampede, which often caused injuries or deaths.

When they reached the cow towns, the herd was sold and the cowboys were paid. It is not surprising that cowboys often went wild, drinking and gambling after 3 long months in the saddle. Lack of law and order was a big problem in early cow towns and cowboys were even banned from Abilene after 1872.

The end of the cowboy era

When the cattle boom ended in 1886–87, the cowboy's life changed a great deal. The invention of wind pumps and barbed wire meant an end to the open range. These inventions also brought an end to fighting between cattlemen and farmers over water and boundaries. Ranches became smaller and were enclosed by fences.

There were no more long drives or 'round ups'. The job of the cowboy was now more of a ranch hand — still helping with cattle, but just as often putting up new fences or repairing old ones. Rules on ranches became much stricter with bans on gambling, drinking and carrying weapons.

The era of the cowboy had lasted only about 30 years.

Topic 3 Cattlemen and cowboys

Use the information provided, your class notes and your textbook to answer the following questions.

1 Complete the timeline by writing the following events in the correct chronological order.

- Barbed wire invented
- American Civil War ended
- A terrible winter killed thousands of cattle
- Cattle ranching began in Texas
- Drought led to grazing problems on the open range
- Joseph McCoy built the first cow town

2 Why did cattlemen in Texas start driving their cattle north to Sedalia after 1865?

3 a How long did these cattle drives take?
b How many cattle were involved?

4 Describe any **two** problems that occurred on these cattle trails.

5 What did some cattlemen begin to do in the 1870s?

1

Date	Event
1830s	
1865	
1867	
1874	
1883	
1886–87	

2

3a

b

4

5

Questions

6 Describe **two** advantages of ranching on the open range.

7 Give **two** reasons why it was easier to start ranching on the Plains in the 1870s than it would have been in the 1860s.

8 Explain **three** factors that led to the end of the open range after 1887.

9 Explain **two** significant ways in which the cattlemen and cowboys contributed to the development of the West.

10 Explain how these developments reduced conflict on the Plains:

a barbed wire

b wind pumps

6

7

8

9

10a

b

Questions

11 Explain briefly how each of these individuals helped the growth of the cattle business:

a Charles Goodnight
b Joseph McCoy
c John Iliff
d Joseph Glidden

12 Describe **three** things that helped the myth of the cowboy to grow.

13 If the cowboy's life was hard and often boring, why did so many men become cowboys? Explain your answer.

11a

b

c

d

12

13

Questions

14 Give **three** examples of how the cowboys' clothing was adapted to their way of life.

15 Why was law and order often a problem in the cow towns?

16 The following key words and phrases are defined in the table. Write each key word next to the correct definition.

- The long drive
- Rustlers
- Abilene
- The open range
- Cattle barons
- Overstocking
- Stampedes
- Riding the line

14

15

16

Definition	Key word or phrase
The owners of the biggest herds on the Plains	
Patrolling the boundaries of the ranch on the open range — a particularly lonely job	
Driving the cattle from the ranch to the railway	
Keeping cattle on the Plains where the land was free and there were no fences	
Having too many cattle on the Plains and not enough grass	
Cattle thieves	
When herds of cattle are panicked into charging	
The first cow town	

Source questions

17 How useful is Source A for showing you what the life of a cowboy was like on the Great Plains? Explain your answer using the source and your own knowledge.

- Quote details from the source to show what you can learn from it about the life of a cowboy — use the provenance (origin) of the source as well.
- Use your knowledge to point out limitations of the source.

Source A

It was the duty of the cowboys to ride swift and tough horses from 12 to 24 hours a day, with rarely a day of rest. They had to guard those cattle at all hours. Hard and bitter work it was. Only the man who has lived the life of those early ranching days can say just how hard and bitter. The vast distances of the country, the loneliness, the days and nights of solitude were hard, but by no means the worst of their difficulties.

Matt Hinkle, a cowboy, describes his life in the 1870s. Quoted in *The American West 1840–1895*, a school history textbook published in 1977

17

Questions

18 Source B gives a different impression of the life of a cowboy compared to Source A. Does Source B prove that the impression of the cowboy's life given in Source A is untrue? Explain your answer using the sources and your own knowledge.

- Do both sources contain truth? If so, why are they different?

Source B

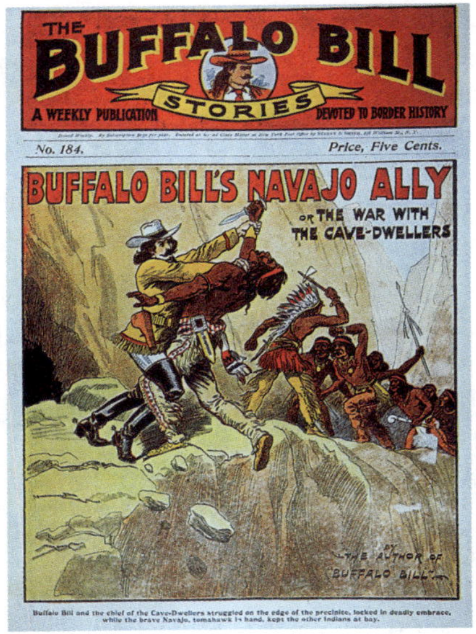

PETER NEWARK'S WESTERN AMERICANA

The cover of a 'dime novel' about William 'Buffalo Bill' Cody, published in the 1890s

18

Extended writing

On separate paper, write a short essay in answer to the following question.

19 In what ways and for what reasons did the life of the cowboy change between the 1860s and 1890?

19 You could include the following in your answer and any other information of your own:

- The long drives to the railway began in the 1860s.
- Cattle ranching spread on to the Plains in the 1870s.
- There was a terrible winter in 1886–87.

Topic 4 The homesteaders

From the mid-1860s to the 1880s, more and more people tried to make their homes on the Plains — land that until 1840 had been called the Great American Desert. There were three main reasons for this rapid increase:

- **The actions of the government.** In 1862, the **Homestead Act** was passed. This offered 65 hectares (160 acres) of free land to anyone building a home and trying to farm the land for 5 years. These settlers were called 'homesteaders'. In 1873, the **Timber and Culture Act** gave settlers another 65 hectares of free land on the condition they planted trees on a quarter of it. The government was also using the army to push the Plains Indians on to smaller reservations. This made more land available to white settlers.
- **The end of the American Civil War in 1865.** This brought freedom to thousands of black families who had been kept as slaves on southern plantations. Many of these people went west, as did thousands of ex-soldiers and their families.
- **The completion of a railway across the continent in 1869.** This is described in more detail in Topic 5, but the railway helped increase the numbers going west in two ways:
  - — As an incentive to build the railway, the government gave the railway companies land on both sides of the railway line. This land was sold off relatively cheaply and advertisements in both the eastern states and Europe attracted thousands of settlers.
  - — After the railway had been completed, it became much easier and safer for people to travel to the West.

Why did people become homesteaders?

Both 'push' and 'pull' factors played a part in bringing homesteaders to the Plains.

Most were **pulled** by the free land offered by the government or the cheap land promised by the railway companies. Some were **pioneers**, drawn by a sense of exploration and adventure and the opportunity to start a new life.

Other homesteaders were **pushed** west by a variety of reasons:

- **Black ex-slaves** were trying to get away from the racism that continued in the South after the Civil War.
- **Religious groups** were trying to escape from religious persecution. For example, many Jews fled from Russia to the Great Plains.
- **Poor whites** were trying to get away from poverty in the eastern states or Europe.

Another thing that drew many to the West was the idea of 'manifest destiny' — the belief that one day the whole American continent would be populated and controlled by white Americans.

Problems on the homesteads

Once they had arrived on the Plains, the homesteaders had many problems to overcome:

- **Building a home**: there were few trees on the Plains and most homesteaders had to live in **sod houses** at first. These homes were cool in summer and warm in winter, but they had many drawbacks: rain came in through the sod roofs; there was usually just one large room with a curtain across to give some privacy; they were impossible to keep clean; bugs and insects were constant problems. By the 1880s, some successful homesteaders were building houses with timber brought from the East by rail.
- **Water**: wells had to be dug to provide fresh water.
- **Fuel**: lack of wood meant that cattle or buffalo dung had to be used for fuel.
- **Loneliness**: in the early days, homesteads might be miles apart and neighbours were not seen often, especially in winter.
- **Farming problems** made it difficult to survive:
  - The hot summers with low rainfall and frequent droughts meant there was a lack of water, which made growing crops difficult.
  - The tough prairie ground was hard to plough with the cast iron ploughs brought from the East.
  - Crops that grew well in the East produced poor yields on the drier Plains.
  - The lack of trees and therefore a shortage of wood for fencing meant that where farms were close to grazing land cattle would wander on to the crops.
  - There were few people around to help gather crops at harvest time.
  - 65 hectares was just not enough land to make a living in such difficult circumstances.
  - Plagues of grasshoppers sometimes destroyed crops completely.

Solutions

Life was always a struggle for these homesteaders and many gave up. However, for those who did survive, various inventions and new ideas from the late 1870s onwards made life easier.

- The development of wind pumps meant that water could be pumped up anywhere from the water table below ground and a new technique called '**dry farming**' helped keep moisture in the soil.
- A steel plough that could cut through the hard prairie soil was invented by John Deere. It became known as the 'sod buster'.
- In 1874, Russian farmers introduced a new type of wheat called **Turkey Red**, which was able to cope better with the harsh growing conditions on the Plains.
- The introduction of barbed wire in 1874 gave farmers a cheap way of fencing in their land and keeping animals off it.
- By 1880, mechanical reapers and threshers had become cheaper, so farming without lots of help became easier.
- The 1873 Timber and Culture Act gave homesteaders more land (see page 32).

By the 1890s, farmers on the Plains had become so successful that they were producing not just enough for their own needs, but a surplus that was being exported to Britain and other countries. Their success was not just the result of new inventions and new ideas. These people had great skill, courage and determination as well as a willingness to adapt to new methods and ideas as they came along. The development of the railway also helped greatly as it made it easier to bring new materials and machinery to the Plains and, later, to send surplus crops to the East and far West.

The role of women

The success of the homesteaders was not only down to the men. They may have built the sod houses, dug the wells and ploughed the land, but the role of their wives was just as important, which included:

- trying to make the sod house into a clean home despite the earth floors and walls
- keeping clothes clean despite the lack of proper soap
- building fires and cooking despite the lack of wood for fuel
- looking after the sick and coping with many pregnancies despite the lack of medicines and doctors
- teaching their children to read and write in the early days when there were no schools
- helping their husbands with the gathering of the harvest

Perhaps most significantly of all, women helped the development of **communities** on the Plains. The cattlemen may have built the first permanent settlements, but the homesteaders and their wives demanded schools, churches, more stores and better law and order. As the homesteaders established themselves on the Plains in growing numbers, Western towns became more peaceful with a strong sense of community, and social gatherings became common.

Gradually, more and more Indian land was opened up to settlers. In 1889, the government bought 2 million acres of land from the Indians and on 22 April 1889 thousands of people gathered on the boundary of this land ready to grab what they could. This **Oklahoma land race** saw the last great rush of white settlers to the Great Plains.

Topic 4 The homesteaders

Use the information provided, your class notes and your textbook to answer the following questions.

1 Complete the timeline by writing the following events in the correct chronological order.

- Timber and Culture Act passed
- Railway across the whole continent completed
- Oklahoma land race
- Farming machinery became cheaper
- Homestead Act passed
- Russian farmers brought Turkey Red wheat to the Plains
- American Civil War ended

2 Explain briefly how each of these things helped increase the numbers of settlers moving west from the 1860s to the 1880s:

a the actions of the government

b the end of the Civil War

c the completion of the trans-continental railway

1

Date	Event
1862	
1865	
1869	
1873	
1874	
1880	
1889	

2a

b

c

Questions

3 What was the main factor that 'pulled' people west after 1862?

4 What attracted the pioneers to the West?

5 What did the settlers have to do to get their free land?

6 Complete the table by giving **one** reason why each group of people became homesteaders, apart from the attraction of free land.

Group	What pushed them west
Black ex-slaves	
Poor whites	
Religious groups	

7 Describe **two** advantages of sod houses.

8 Describe **three** disadvantages of sod houses.

9 Describe any **four** important roles women had on the Plains.

10 How did the presence of women and families help the development of peaceful communities on the Plains?

Questions

11 Complete the table by describing the farming problems homesteaders experienced and how each problem was eventually solved. Two examples have been inserted for you. Note: one problem you will describe was not solved before 1895.

12 Describe **two** other things, apart from farming problems, that made life hard for homesteaders and their families.

13 What personal qualities helped some homesteaders to be more successful than others?

11

Farming problem	Eventual solution
Crops that grew well in the East produced poor yields on the Plains	
	The 1873 Timber and Culture Act gave homesteaders more land

12

13

14 Which development did more to help the homesteaders succeed: the railway or farming inventions?

14

Source A

CORBIS

A family outside their sod house in Nebraska around 1890

Source B

BRIDGEMAN

A picture painted by Fanny Palmer in 1868

Source questions

15 What does Source A tell you about life on the Plains?

- Do not just describe what you see in the source. Try to make deductions about the lives of the people based on what you can see.

15

Questions

16 What different impression of life on the Plains do you get from Source B compared to Source A?

- You must explain *how* they differ, not why.
- Compare details in *both* sources — do not just describe one.

17 Why do you think Sources A and B give such different impressions of life on the Plains? Explain your answer using the sources and your own knowledge.

- You need to give *reasons* for the differences. Do not repeat *how* the sources differ.

Extended writing

On separate paper, write a short essay in answer to the following question.

18 Who contributed more to the development of the West by 1890: the homesteaders or the cattlemen and cowboys?

16

17

18

Guidelines

A very good answer will include:

- examples of how *both* the homesteaders *and* cattlemen and cowboys contributed to the development of the West
- a clear conclusion with an answer to the question set, backed up with a sound reason and accurate knowledge

Topic 5 The railway

During the 1840s and 1850s, the journey west by wagon train or stage coach was slow and sometimes dangerous. All this changed with the building of the trans-continental railroad.

The government was particularly keen to see a railway built across the country, mainly for business and political reasons:

- It would improve trade links with eastern countries like China and lead to the development of ports on the western coast of America.
- It would create a greater sense of national unity if the eastern and western sides of the country could be linked more effectively; help to fulfil the belief in 'manifest destiny'; and improve law and order and government in the western territories.

Building the railway

Consequently, in 1862 the **Central Pacific** Company started building eastwards from California, while the **Union Pacific** Company began building westwards from Omaha, Nebraska. Many difficult problems had to be overcome during the building of the railway:

- The Central Pacific Company accomplished great feats of engineering as its line had to cross deep canyons and go through the Rocky Mountains.
- Thousands of labourers were needed — many of these were Irish and Chinese immigrants.
- The cost was great. Most of the money came from the government in the form of loans, but it also gave about 30 km of land on both sides of the tracks to the rail companies as an incentive to keep on building. This meant they eventually owned about 150 million acres of land on the Great Plains. Later, the rail companies sold off this land cheaply to homesteaders — partly for immediate profits, but also for long-term benefits. The more settlers they could attract to the West to live and work, the more demand there would be for both passenger and freight services. A huge poster campaign promising cash discounts and special loan terms was launched in both America and Europe. This encouraged even more people to travel to the American West.

Despite these problems, the task was completed and the two lines met at **Promontory Point** in Utah in 1869. In 1870, its first full year in operation, 15,000 people travelled on the railroad. By 1882, 1 million people were travelling on it, some in the luxury of first-class trains that could travel from New York to San Francisco in 4 days. However, most people made the journey in third class on slower trains with hard, wooden seats, which took 10 days.

Effects on the development of the West

- **The cattle business** was greatly stimulated by the railway. Cattlemen began their trail drives from Texas in the 1860s to reach the railway. This led to the building of cow towns. Later, cattle ranches spread to the Plains to make the journey to the railway easier.

- **Homesteaders** came west in greater numbers because the railway made travel so much easier. Supplies of timber and machinery could be brought more easily by rail and this helped to improve farming on the Plains.
- **Trade** increased because of the railway. It was easier for people in the West to get more supplies from the East and easier for cattlemen and farmers to send their products east. Foreign trade also increased.
- **Law and order** improved because judges and lawmen could travel around more easily. This led to the growth of more peaceful, settled communities by 1890.
- **The Native Americans** were affected badly by the railway. First, it frightened off the buffalo, which meant the Indians had to move camp. Later, it brought buffalo hunters. Buffalo hides became valuable because they could be made into high-quality leather goods in the eastern USA. Over 1 million hides were shipped by rail to the East in just 3 years, from 1872 to 1874, and this continued into the 1880s. Special excursion trains were even run by some companies for sport and shooting buffalo through the windows of a moving train became a popular pastime. The railway was also bringing more and more settlers to the West and this, too, helped speed up the end of the Indian way of life.
- **The growth of cities** in the West such as Denver, Dallas and Los Angeles was encouraged by the development of the railway network. By 1890, the railway boom was helping America to become one of the richest nations in the world.

Conclusion

The above points show that the railway played an important role in the development of the American West. Between 1850 and 1890 the amount of railway track grew from about 20,000 km to about 324,000 km. Most of this was in the West. The difficulties and dangers described in Topic 2 that were faced by the early travellers became a thing of the past.

Topic 5 The railway

Use the information provided, your class notes and your textbook to answer the following questions.

1 Describe **three** problems that had to be overcome when building the railway across the USA.

2 Give **two** reasons why the government was so keen to see the railway built.

3 How did the government help in the building of the railway?

4 Complete the table by explaining clearly how the railway either improved or worsened the way of life of each group of people.

5 Describe **two** other ways in which the railway helped the growth of the USA.

1

2

3

4

Group	How the railway affected them
Cattlemen and cowboys	
Homesteaders	
Law officials	
Native Americans	

5

Questions

Source question

6 What can you learn from Sources A and B about the effects of the railway on the development of the Plains?

- Use *both* sources in your answer.
- Do not just describe what you can see — explain how it affected life on the Plains.

Source A

A map showing the railway moving west

Source B

PETER NEWARK'S WESTERN AMERICANA

Men shooting buffalo from a train

6

Extended writing

On separate paper, write a short essay in answer to the following question.

7 'The railway was by far the most important reason for the successful development of the West by 1895.' How far do you agree with this statement? Explain your answer.

7 You could include the following in your answer and any other information of your own:

- The mountain men helped guide early wagon trains through the Rocky Mountains.
- In 1869, the building of the trans-continental railway was completed.
- By the 1880s, farm machinery was brought to the Plains by rail.

Topic 6 Law and order

When white people began to move west in the 1840s and 1850s, there was no organised system of law and order. Gradually, the government set up the following system:

- **In towns**: town marshals were appointed to sort out problems like fighting and gambling.
- **In counties**: the county sheriff and his deputies enforced the law.
- **In a territory**: the highest official was the US marshal, who was appointed by the president. The territories were so large that he was helped by deputies.
- **Judges** travelled around, hearing cases and passing sentences.

Despite this system, law and order remained a big problem in the period 1860–90 for the following reasons:

- The West was a huge area and it took time to organise the system properly. Decisions made in the capital, Washington, took a long time to take effect in the West.
- Before the railway came, travel was slow and it was difficult for marshals and judges to reach some areas.
- Lawmen were not well paid and it was difficult to get people to do the job. Sometimes, ex-criminals like **Wyatt Earp** became town marshals. Earp brought Dodge City under control in the 1870s, but he was criticised for using ruthless methods.

Vigilantes

Because of these difficulties, people sometimes tried to enforce law and order themselves by creating their own groups or committees of vigilance (vigilantes). These were ordinary people, often leading citizens, who got together to catch and punish criminals. **Vigilantes** often dealt effectively with real criminals and were welcomed by many people at first. However, they rarely bothered to give people a fair hearing and many innocent people suffered at their hands. In time, they became more feared than the criminals.

Problem areas

Problems were most common in three areas: mining towns, cow towns and the Plains.

- **Mining towns**: these towns grew rapidly during the gold rush — too rapidly for a proper system of justice to be created. There were many quarrels between miners over ownership claims of places where gold was found. The towns also attracted criminal types, gamblers and prostitutes, all anxious to part successful miners from their money.
  Solutions: miners set up their own miners' courts, where ordinary miners heard disputes and settled them. These courts were often successful in settling claim-jumping disputes, but it was 'rough justice' with no means of appeal for people who felt they had been treated badly. Vigilantes usually dealt with cases of theft or murder, often in a crude and brutal manner, such as by lynching (hanging) the accused without a trial.
- **Cow towns**: places like Abilene and Dodge City often had problems with cowboys. These towns marked the end of the long drives where the cattle were sold. After two or three hard months on the trail, the cowboys were paid their wages and wanted to

have a good time in the bars and gambling houses. As in the mining towns, the presence of men with money attracted criminal types and fights were commonplace. Town marshals were not well paid and seldom stayed in the job for long. **Solutions**: as more homesteaders and their families moved into the area, demand for better law and order increased. Problems in cow towns were eventually solved by banning guns and, in Abilene after 1872, banning cowboys. New, strict laws were enforced by tough lawmen like Wyatt Earp in Dodge City and 'Wild Bill' Hickok in Abilene.

- **The Plains**: there was conflict between cattlemen and homesteaders. Lack of fencing meant fights were common over such things as:
  - disputes over land boundaries — where one person's land ended and another's began
  - cattle eating or trampling on crops
  - water holes and rivers — water was scarce and there were often disputes

  One of the worst fights between cattlemen and homesteaders was the **Johnson County War** in Wyoming in 1892. Cattlemen accused the farmers of rustling (stealing) cattle and hired gunmen from Texas to drive homesteaders out of the state. This failed but none of the cattlemen were brought to trial. **Solutions**: in the end, new inventions brought peace to the quarrels between cattlemen and homesteaders. The wind pump stopped fights over water because anyone could draw up all the water they needed on their own land. Barbed wire brought an end to disputes over land and stopped cattle going on to farmland.

Criminals

Some women became criminals. **Belle Starr** took part in robberies and rustled cattle and horses. She was sentenced to 5 years in prison and was eventually shot in the back in 1889. **Etta Place** was a partner of Harry '**The Sundance Kid**' Longbaugh. Together with **Butch Cassidy**, they robbed banks and trains.

These outlaws, and others like William '**Billy the Kid**' Bonney, were all real people, but the 'dime novels' written in the 1880s and 1890s for people in the East often exaggerated and glamorised their activities. The Johnson County War showed that even in the 1890s conflict between cattlemen and farmers could flare up, although some western states like Montana and Oregon had few major problems with law and order.

Achieving law and order

By 1895, effective law and order had been brought to the 'wild' areas. This was the result of a number of factors:

- Disputes ended between cattlemen and homesteaders.
- Families increased the demand for law and order.
- The railway network developed.
- The Native Americans were confined to reservations, so fighting between whites and Indians ended.
- When the population of a territory reached 60,000, the people could apply for it to become a full state of the union. When territories became full states, they took on the responsibility for law and order locally, so important decisions were made more quickly.

Topic 6 Law and order

Use the information provided, your class notes and your textbook to answer the following questions.

1 Describe the roles of the following people in the system of law and order that the government set up in the West:
a town marshals
b county sheriffs
c US marshals
d judges

2 Give **three** reasons why there were problems with law and order despite this system.

3 a Why did some people become vigilantes?
b How effective were they at maintaining order?

4 Why were there problems in mining towns?

5 How did miners try to solve their problems of law and order?

1a

b

c

d

2

3a

b

4

5

Questions

6 How successful were the solutions of the miners?

7 Why was there a lack of order in the cow towns?

8 How was this problem in cow towns solved?

9 Describe **two** things that caused conflict between cattlemen and homesteaders.

10 What inventions helped solved these problems?

11 Name two women who became criminals in the West.

12 What does the Johnson County War tell us about law and order in the West in the 1890s?

13 Complete the table using the words and phrases below. Two examples have been inserted for you.

- Cowboys and townspeople
- Ownership of water rights
- On the Plains
- Drinking, fighting and gambling
- Ownership of land
- Fences and wind pumps
- Miners' courts
- Banning cowboys from towns
- Rustling cattle
- Claim jumping
- Miners and other miners
- Mining towns
- Cow towns
- Tough marshals and sheriffs
- Behaviour of cowboys at end of cattle drives
- Cattlemen and homesteaders
- Lynchings by vigilantes
- Drinking, fighting and gambling

13

Where were the problems?	Who did the problems involve?	What were the problems over?	How were the problems solved?
■	■	■ ■	■ Miners' courts ■
■	■	■ Behaviour of cowboys at end of cattle drives ■	■ ■
■	■	■ ■ ■	■

Questions

Source question

14 Is Source A an accurate interpretation of life in a Western town before 1895? Explain your answer using the source and your own knowledge.

- Could the source be accurate in some respects and inaccurate in others?
- Support any points you make by referring to details in the source and/or your own knowledge.

Extended writing

On separate paper, write a short essay in answer to the following question.

15 'It was the increasing numbers of women and families that made the West more peaceful by 1895.' How far would you agree with this statement? Explain your answer.

Source A

PETER NEWARK'S WESTERN AMERICANA

'In Without Knocking' by Charles Russell, painted in 1909. Russell worked on cattle ranches between 1880 and 1892

14

15

Guidelines

A very good answer will include:

- examples of how *both* women and families *and* other factors helped make the West more peaceful
- a clear conclusion which contains an opinion as to their comparative importance, backed up with a sound reason and accurate knowledge

Topic 7 The Plains wars

In 1834, the Great Plains were given to the Native Americans by the government. The territory was thought to be of no use to white people because of the harsh climate — bitterly cold winters and baking hot summers — and a lack of trees and a scarcity of water. It was believed by all who saw it that growing crops would be impossible and they called the area the **Great American Desert**. It would be Indian country 'as long as the stars shall shine and the rivers flow'.

However, by 1895 all their lands had been taken from them and the Indians were forced to live on small, tightly controlled **reservations**.

Early 1840s to mid-1860s

The first whites to go west — the mountain men, the settlers going to Oregon and California, and the Mormons — were not planning to settle on the Plains, so there was little trouble with Native Americans. However, after the Californian gold rush of 1848–49, the number of whites going through Indian Territory increased greatly. The Indians began to feel as though they were being invaded and sometimes attacked miners and wagon trains. The government started to send soldiers to protect travellers, and fear and suspicion grew.

In the **Treaty of Fort Laramie** (1851) the Indians were persuaded to move on to smaller areas of land. They were given a promise that no whites would enter these areas. In return, the Indians agreed to stop attacking travellers.

This treaty was soon broken by whites. Ten years later, another treaty was drawn up based on a new policy, which was to push the Indians on to even smaller areas of land called reservations.

When gold was discovered in Montana in 1862, whites poured into the area along a new trail, the Bozeman Trail, which again passed through Indian Territory. The whole Indian way of life seemed threatened and some tribes began to fight back. The result was the **Plains Wars** of 1862–76. During this conflict, there were many terrible attacks by Indians on white settlers and wagon trains. There were equally terrible attacks by soldiers on Native Americans, such as the **Sand Creek Massacre** of 1864 and the attack on the Cheyenne at the **Battle of Washita River** in 1868.

Why did white attitudes change?

- By the 1860s, the government had decided that the land on the Plains was not useless and was needed for white settlers. The army needed to protect white settlers on the Plains.
- There was also a desire for revenge after Native American attacks on whites. Some army chiefs, like General Sheridan (quoted as saying 'The only good Indians I ever saw were dead'), wanted all Indians to be wiped out. They have sometimes been called 'the exterminators'.
- Slaughter of the Indians was mainly linked to the idea of '**manifest destiny**'. The government was anxious to see all

lands between the Atlantic and Pacific Oceans under white American control. The Indians were seen as an obstacle to achieving this as they did not cultivate or develop the land in any way. Some whites, known as 'humanitarians', believed Indians should be treated with respect and that the problem could be solved peacefully. Their aim was to teach the Native Americans how to grow crops, and how to read and write — in effect, how to adopt the 'white' way of life.

The Battle of the Little Bighorn

One of the few Native American tribes to get the better of the army up to 1868 was the **Sioux**. In a second **Treaty of Fort Laramie** (1868), the government promised that white settlers would never be allowed into the Black Hills of Dakota. This was to be the Great Sioux reservation and was sacred land to the Sioux. The government also promised to stop the development of the Bozeman Trail and to close three army forts there.

This treaty was also broken. In 1874, gold was discovered in the Black Hills and thousands of miners swarmed in and staked claims to Sioux land.

The government tried to buy the Black Hills, but the Sioux were not interested in selling. As a result, they were ordered to leave the territory. Instead, they gathered in huge numbers in the Valley of the Little Bighorn River. In the summer of 1876, the army was ordered to attack.

The plan was to have three columns of soldiers converge on the Indian camp simultaneously from three directions: one led by Colonel Gibbon from the west; one led by General Crook from the south; and a third led by General Terry — accompanied by General Custer — from the east. However, Crook's column was attacked and he was forced to retreat.

Terry then ordered Custer to take the 7th Cavalry to the south of the Wolf Mountains and then to turn north towards Little Bighorn. However, Custer decided to cut across the mountains and arrived a day early. He divided his troops into three groups and attacked immediately. Custer's group of around 225 men came up against a force led by **Sitting Bull** and **Crazy Horse**. The soldiers took up their position on a ridge where the 'last stand' took place. Custer and his men were all killed.

Reasons for Custer's defeat

Custer was partly to blame for this defeat:

- He divided his force, thus weakening it, before making his attack.
- He turned down Terry's offer of Gatling guns (machine guns).
- He did not keep to the original plan and attacked without waiting for the rest of the forces led by Generals Gibbon and Terry.

Custer was known to be an ambitious man. Some said he hoped one day to run for president. It is possible that he hoped to get all the glory of victory at the battle for himself. However, other factors also played a part in his defeat:

- It was unusual to find so many Indians (about 2,000 warriors) in one place.
- Indians did not normally stand and fight when faced with a

cavalry charge. From his previous experience of fighting Indians, Custer must have expected them to scatter.

- The Indians were well armed with Winchester repeating rifles.

Consequences of Little Bighorn

The Indians may have won this battle but they suffered badly after it. Custer's defeat shocked all white Americans and large forces of soldiers were sent west. Within a short time, the Sioux and all other tribes were rounded up and forced on to reservations. There were four main reasons for the ultimate defeat of the Plains Indians:

- By the early 1880s, there were few buffalo left on the Plains due to the **buffalo hunters**, who were only interested in skins and left the bodies of dead buffalo to rot. This hunting played a big part in ending the resistance of the Indians because it destroyed their main source of food and all the other things their lives depended on. Consequently, they became increasingly dependent on the government for food supplies.
- The forces against them were too great. They could not resist the hundreds of well-armed, professional soldiers sent in after Little Bighorn who pursued them even in the winter months when they rapidly ran short of food supplies and became demoralised.
- The government was determined to achieve 'manifest destiny' — complete control of all the lands of America. The Plains Indians were not going to be allowed to stand in the way of this scheme.
- The Indian tribes never combined forces against the army. The Battle of Little Bighorn showed what was possible when large numbers of Indians fought together. However, it was not part of Indian culture for different tribes to support one another.

Life was very hard on the reservations. Native Americans were forced to obey the laws of the USA instead of their own tribal laws. They were made to live like white people, including changing their religion and the way they dressed. The **Dawes Act** of 1887 broke up the reservations into smaller areas, the idea being that each Indian family would be given their own piece of land to cultivate. However, many Indians rejected their plots and others sold them off cheaply to whites. By 1905, all Indian Territory had been opened up to white settlement.

In 1890, an Indian called **Wovoka** told other Indians about a vision he had had. This foretold that whites would leave Indian lands, the Indian dead would return and so would the buffalo. To help bring this about, Indians had to perform the '**ghost dance**'. Sadly, this led to a tragedy at **Wounded Knee**. Worried about the ghost dance, soldiers tried to disarm a band of Sioux. When they resisted, the soldiers opened fire and 153 Sioux men, women and children were killed.

It was the last sad event in the story of the Native Americans. Manifest destiny had been achieved. The West was won.

Topic 7 The Plains wars

Use the information provided, your class notes and your textbook to answer the following questions.

1 Why was there little trouble between Indians and whites in the 1830s and early 1840s?

2 Why did whites refer to the Great Plains as the Great American Desert?

3 Why did problems between Indians and the government increase after 1849?

4 What was agreed in the Treaty of Fort Laramie, 1851?

5 What was the policy of the government towards the Native Americans after 1861?

6 What was the idea of 'manifest destiny'?

7 Give **two** other reasons to explain why the attitudes of the government towards the Indians had changed so much by the 1860s.

8 Explain the different solutions to the Indian 'problem' put forward by
a 'exterminators'
b 'humanitarians'

1

2

3

4

5

6

7

8a

b

Questions

9 What were the Sioux promised in the treaty of 1868?

10 How was this treaty broken in 1874?

11 How did the government try to solve the problem of the Black Hills at first?

12 Why were soldiers sent to the Black Hills in 1876?

13 Describe briefly the US Army's plan of attack on the Native Americans at Little Bighorn.

14 Give **three** reasons explaining why General Custer was to blame for his defeat.

15 Describe **three** other factors that helped bring about Custer's defeat.

16 Was the Battle of the Little Bighorn really a victory for the Indians in the long term?

9

10

11

12

13

14

15

16

Questions

17 What events led up to the massacre at Wounded Knee in 1890?

18 Explain how each of the following factors helped bring about the final defeat of the Plains Indians:

a the US Army

b the idea of 'manifest destiny'

c the destruction of the buffalo

d lack of unity among the Native American tribes

17

18a

b

c

d

19 Complete the timeline by writing the following events in the correct chronological order.

- Army massacre of Native Americans at Sand Creek
- Custer's 7th Cavalry defeated at the Battle of the Little Bighorn
- Government declared the Great Plains to be Indian territory for all time
- Massacre of Sioux Indians at Wounded Knee
- Gold rush to California brought more whites into Indian territory
- Dawes Act broke up the reservations into smaller plots
- Discovery of gold brought whites into the Black Hills of Dakota
- First Treaty of Fort Laramie
- Second Treaty of Fort Laramie
- Bozeman Trail developed after gold discovered in Montana

19

Date	Event
1834	
1848–49	
1851	
1862	
1864	
1868	
1874	
1876	
1887	
1890	

Questions

Source questions

20 How useful is Source A to someone trying to explain the conflict between Indians and whites between 1860 and 1895? Explain your answer using the source and your own knowledge.

- Refer to details in the picture and to the origin of the source to show how it is useful.
- Use your knowledge of other reasons for the conflict to explain how the value of the source is limited.
- Sum up your answer with a clear, brief conclusion.

Source A

PETER NEWARK'S WESTERN AMERICANA

A picture created by a white man in 1892

20

Questions

21 Do you think Source B is an accurate interpretation of the Battle of the Little Bighorn? Explain your answer using the source and your own knowledge.

- Could the source be accurate in some respects but inaccurate in others?
- Support any points you make by referring to details in the source and/or your background knowledge.

Extended writing

On separate paper, write a short essay in answer to the following question.

22 How important was the destruction of the buffalo by white hunters in the weakening of the traditional way of life of the Plains Indians between 1876 and 1895?

PETER NEWARK'S WESTERN AMERICANA

Source B

'Custer's Last Stand' by Edgar Paxson, 1899. Paxson did many years of research before creating this painting

21

22 You could include the following in your answer and any other information of your own:

- The buffalo was the main source of food for Native Americans.
- The consequences of the Battle of the Little Bighorn.
- The Dawes Act of 1887.

Topic 8 Overview

This enquiry in depth focuses on the development of the American West in general and the area of the Great Plains in particular. In 1840, this area was known to early travellers as the Great American Desert, fit only for Native Americans and buffalo. There were no towns, no organised transport system, and no system of law and order or government apart from informal systems that existed in the tribes who had lived on the Plains for hundreds of years.

However, by 1895 the Plains had stable, fast-growing towns, a developing railway system, organised state governments, and huge areas of land under cultivation. They were home to hundreds of thousands of white settlers, including many from Europe. Incredibly, these dramatic changes had happened in just 55 years.

How were the changes achieved?

This book has been about those changes and the people who brought them into being: miners, cattlemen, cowboys, homesteaders and lawmen. Their ability to adapt to this difficult environment, as well as their courage and determination, played a huge part in the transformation of the Plains. They were also greatly helped by other factors:

- the development of the railway which made it much easier for people and goods to travel to and from the West
- technological inventions such as wind pumps
- the determination of the government to see the country united and the idea of 'manifest destiny' fulfilled

What problems were there?

However, there were many problems along the way before these tremendous changes were achieved:

- In the early days, thousands died on the journey west.
- Before a proper system of law and order was established, many people died in clashes between whites in mining towns, cow towns and on the Plains.
- Racism towards minority groups like Chinese and Mexican migrant workers was evident in many Western communities.
- Worst of all, there was the systematic and often brutal destruction of the Plains Indians and their way of life.

Conclusion

The fact that all these things happened simultaneously over a period of just 55 years is difficult to grasp. The first task in this topic will help you to appreciate how the various changes described in this book happened side by side. The final tasks will remind you of some of the key individuals and places in the story of the American West.

Topic 8 Overview

Use the information provided, your class notes and your textbook to answer the following questions.

1 All the labels shown in this table are in the correct column but not in the correct chronological order. Complete the table on pages 62–63 by writing each event in the correct place. Three examples have been inserted for you in the correct places to get you started.

Plains Indians	The first white people in the West	Cattlemen and cowboys
US government begins to push Indians on to reservations	Gold discovered in Black Hills; Brigham Young dies	Cattlemen begin to build ranches on the Plains; cattle boom begins
Ghost dance and final tragedy at Wounded Knee	Mountain Meadows Massacre; gold discovered in Colorado and Nevada	Cattle boom ends following overgrazing and bad winter
The Plains wars between the US Army and Indians begin	Utah becomes a full state of the USA	Ranches smaller, producing fewer but better animals; cowboys become more of a ranch hand
Only Indians and buffalo live on the Great Plains	Gold discovered in Montana; Bozeman Trail opened up in Indian Territory	Cattle ranching develops in Texas
Almost all buffalo gone; all Indians on reservations	Farmers, miners and Mormons travel west	Too many cattle in Texas — price of beef falls; trail drives to the railway begin
General Custer defeated by the Sioux at Little Bighorn	Salt Lake City very prosperous; Mormon community flourishes	Beef becomes more popular; price of beef rises and Texan ranchers do well

Questions

The homesteaders	The railway	Law and order
Timber and Culture Act gives more land to homesteaders; Turkey Red wheat introduced	Railway helps to make the USA the world's leading producer of farming and industrial goods	Johnson County War — the last big outbreak of lawlessness in the West
Wind pumps and barbed wire help stop fighting between cattlemen and homesteaders	Travel by stage coach is the fastest form of transport to the West	Tough sheriffs like Wyatt Earp bring peace to cow towns
No farming on the Plains — thought to be the Great American Desert	Rail links all across the West make travel much easier	Problems of law and order in the mining towns — miners' courts and vigilantes
Homestead Act passed — 65 hectares of free land made available to settlers	Thousands of buffalo hides transported east by rail	Fighting on the Plains between farmers and cattlemen over land and water
Homesteaders begin to move on to the eastern edge of the low Plains	Travel to the West is by wagon train	Joseph McCoy builds first cow town at Abilene; lack of law and order in cow towns
Most of the Great Plains used for wheat production; most homesteaders doing well	The railway across USA completed at Promontory Point in Utah	Problems with vigilantes in mining towns in Nevada

1

Date	Plains Indians	The first white people in the West	Cattlemen and cowboys
1840s			
1850s			Beef becomes more popular; price of beef rises and Texan ranchers do well
1860s			
1870s			
1880s		Salt Lake City very prosperous; Mormon community flourishes	
1890s			

Questions

Date	The homesteaders	The railway	Law and order
1840s			
1850s			Problems with vigilantes in mining towns in Nevada
1860s			
1870s			
1880s			
1890s			

2 Who am I? Write the names of the individuals from the following list to whom each quote refers in the spaces provided:

- Wovoka
- General Custer
- Joseph Smith
- Joseph McCoy
- Wyatt Earp
- Sitting Bull
- Joseph Glidden
- Brigham Young
- John Iliff
- 'Buffalo Bill' Cody

3 Where did it happen? Write the correct place names from the following list in the spaces provided:

- Texas
- Oklahoma
- Ohio
- California
- Mountain Meadows
- Abilene
- Wounded Knee
- Reservations
- Promontory Point
- Johnson County

2a 'I built the first cow town in the 1860s.' ……………………

b 'I started the Mormon Church in 1830.' ……………………

c 'I was defeated by the Sioux at the Little Bighorn in 1876.' ……………………

d 'I led the Mormons to the Salt Lake Valley in the 1840s.' ……………………

e 'I was one of the first cattlemen to start ranching on the High Plains.' ……………………

f 'I invented barbed wire in 1874.' ……………………

g 'My "Wild West" show toured America and Europe.' ……………………

h 'I was a criminal myself before I became marshal of Dodge City.' ……………………

i 'My warriors defeated the US Army at the Little Bighorn.' ……………………

j 'My vision sparked off the "ghost dance" in 1890.' ……………………

3a Gold was discovered here in 1848, leading to the 'gold rush'. ……………………

b The Mormons tried to build their first community in this state. ……………………

c A wagon train was attacked here by Mormons in 1857. ……………………

d Cattle ranching developed here between 1830 and 1865. ……………………

e This was the name of the first ever 'cow town'. ……………………

f This is where the railways linking east and west met in 1869. ……………………

g A 'race' between the settlers occurred here in 1889 to grab Indian land. ……………………

h All Indians lived on these by 1890. ……………………

i This is where many Indians were massacred in 1890. ……………………

j A 'war' was fought here in 1892 between cattlemen and homesteaders. ……………………